NATIONAL
GEOGRAPHIC

School Publishing

Comparing Sizes and Weights

James Nguyen

PICTURE CREDITS

Illustrations by Gaston Vanzet (4–5, 14–15).
All photographs by Lindsay Edwards Photography.

Produced through the worldwide resources of the National Geographic Society, John M. Fahey, Jr., President and Chief Executive Officer; Gilbert M. Grosvenor, Chairman of the Board; Nina D. Hoffman, Executive Vice President and President, Books and Education Publishing Group.

PREPARED BY NATIONAL GEOGRAPHIC SCHOOL PUBLISHING

Ericka Markman, Senior Vice President and President Children's Books and Education Publishing Group; Steve Mico, Senior Vice President and Publisher; Marianne Hiland, Editorial Director; Lynnette Brent, Executive Editor; Michael Murphy and Barbara Wood, Senior Editors; Bea Jackson, Design Director; David Dumo, Art Director; Margaret Sidlowsky, Illustrations Director; Matt Wascavage, Manager of Publishing Services; Sean Philpotts, Production Manager.

MANUFACTURING AND QUALITY MANAGEMENT

Christopher A. Liedel, Chief Financial Officer; Phillip L. Schlosser, Director; Clifton M. Brown III, Manager.

BOOK DEVELOPMENT

Ibis for Kids Australia Pty Limited.

Published by the National Geographic Society
1145 17th Street, N.W.
Washington, D.C. 20036-4688

ISBN 0-7922-6066-X

Fifth Printing 2008
Printed in China

Contents

Pig
heavy animal

Bear
heavier animal

Elephant
heaviest animal

small book

smaller book

smallest book

long table

There are many ways to compare things.
Which things are small? Which things are long?

5

Small Things

Some things are small.
You can compare how small they are.

The book
is **small**.

The crayon
is **smaller** than
the book.

Big

Big is the opposite
of small.

small
ball

big
ball

The penny
is the **smallest**.

Tall Things

Some things are tall.
You can compare how tall they are.

The bookcase is **tall**.

The man
is **taller** than
the bookcase.

The door
is the **tallest**.

Short
Short is the opposite
of tall.

tall glass

short glass

Long Things

Some things are long.
You can compare how long they are.

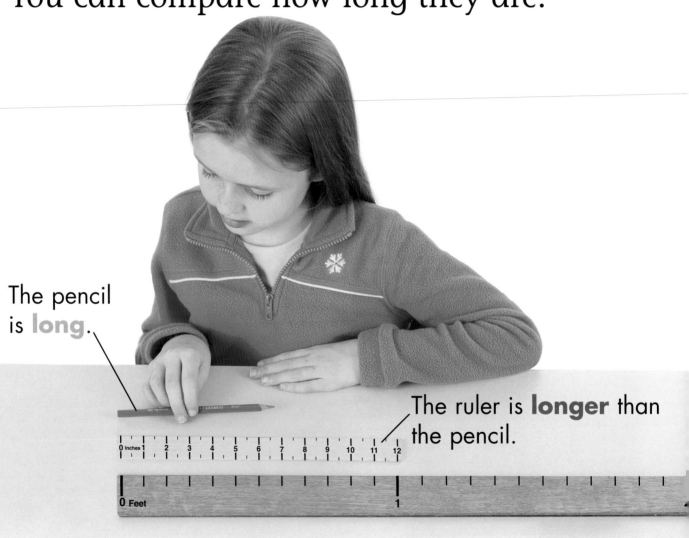

The pencil is **long**.

The ruler is **longer** than the pencil.

Short

Short is the opposite of long.

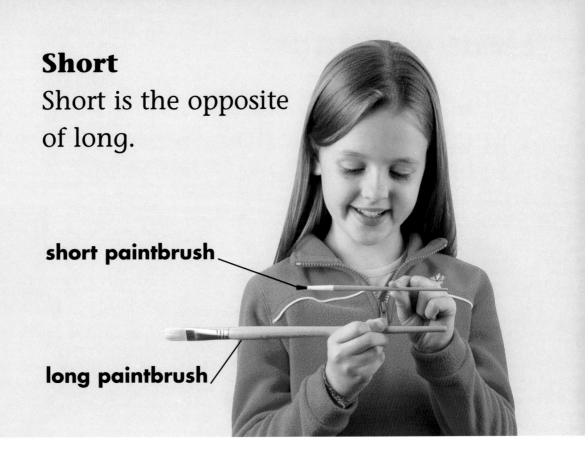

short paintbrush

long paintbrush

The yardstick is the **longest**.

Heavy Things

Some things are heavy.
You can compare how heavy they are.

The book is **heavy**.

The plant is **heavier** than the book.

The backpack is the **heaviest**.

Light
Light is the opposite of heavy.

light box

heavy box

bag

backpack

bench

ball

14

tree

balloon

dog

heavy

heavier

heaviest

long

longer

longest

small

smaller

smallest

tall

taller

tallest

15

Picture Glossary

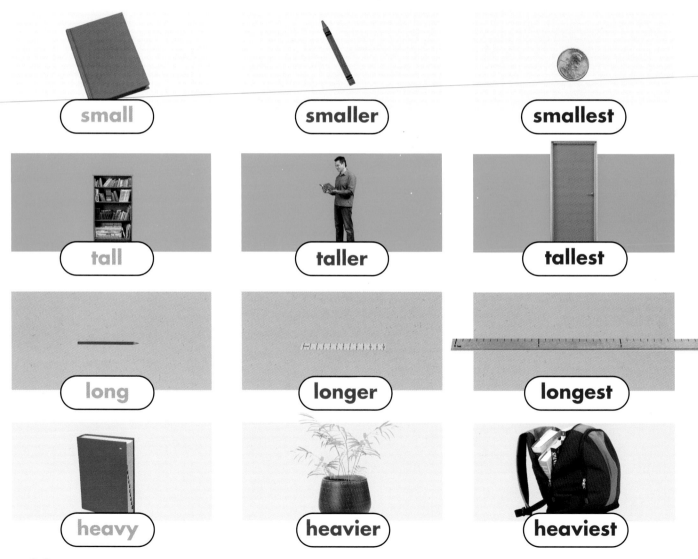

small	smaller	smallest
tall	taller	tallest
long	longer	longest
heavy	heavier	heaviest